Presented To:

By:

Date:

Where Jesus Is

30 Reflections of Christ to Carry with You

FRAN ROGERS

Designed by

Kourtney Axelberg

Contents

Life - 16

Kindness - 17

Wisdom - 18

Mercy - 19

Blessing - 20

Victory - 21

Fellowship - 22

Fruit - 23

Rest - 24

Authority - 25

Light - 26

Abundance - 27

Gentleness - 28

Salvation - 29

Praise - 30

Introduction

The seed for this little book was planted years ago when I began to see the gift God had given our granddaughter, Kourtney. Now, after years of training as a graphic designer, she is combining her gift with the blessing of God's Word.

Jesus, the Living Word, gave Himself for us that He may live in us and we may live in Him (1 Jn 4:9).

Daily memorization and meditations on the person and work of Jesus Christ change the lives of the youngest to the oldest of God's children. When Jesus dwells within our hearts (Eph. 3:17), His nature and disposition are reflected in our thoughts, words, and actions. Others will see and hear Him through us.

Through this little book, we pray His Word will speak to and through His people to a world that desperately needs Him.

Fran Rogers
Father and Family Books
July 2021

Example: After reading the verse for "LOVE," start the morning with the first phrase, "Hold fast" and sense what we are to "hold." Throughout the morning, rehearse the first phrase, then add the second. Continue through the day and connect each phrase. End your day with the whole verse and praise Him for giving you eternal life in Him.

Each word takes on its own meaning yet is joined to the others to form the thoughts and image our Father has planned to work in us.

THERE

IS

Love

"Hold fast
the pattern of sound words
which you have heard from me,
in faith and love
which are in Christ Jesus."
2 Timothy 1:13

THERE
IS

Joy

"These things
I have spoken to you,
that My joy may remain in you,
and that your joy may be full."
John 15:11

THERE
IS

Peace

"Therefore,
having been justified by faith,
we have peace with God
through our Lord Jesus Christ."
Romans 5:1

THERE
IS

Patience

"Now may the Lord direct your hearts
into the love of God
and into the patience of Christ."
2 Thessalonians 3:5

THERE
IS

Comfort

"Now may the God of patience
and comfort grant you to be
like-minded toward one another,
according to Christ Jesus."
Romans 15:5

THERE
IS

Faith

"I live by faith in the Son of God,
who loved me and gave Himself for me."
Galatians 2:20

THERE
IS

Truth

"I am the way, the truth, and the life.
No one comes to the Father
except through Me."
John 14:6

THERE
IS

Grace

"And of His fullness
we have all received,
and grace for grace."
John 1:16

THERE
IS

Righteousness

"For He made Him
who knew no sin to be sin for us,
that we might become the
righteousness of God in Him."
2 Corinthians 5:21

THERE

IS

Hope

"To them God willed to make known
what are the riches of the glory
of this mystery among the Gentiles:
which is Christ in you, the hope of glory."
Colossians 1:27

THERE
IS

Forgiveness

"In Him we have redemption
through His blood,
the forgiveness of sins,
according to the riches of His grace."
Ephesians 1:7

THERE

IS

Promise

"From this man's seed,
according to the promise,
God raised up for Israel
a Savior—Jesus"
Acts 13:23

THERE
IS

Strength

"I can do all things through Christ
who strengthens me."
Philippians 4:13

THERE

IS

Completeness

"And you are complete in Him, who is
the head of all principality and power."
Colossians 2:10

THERE
IS

Liberty

"Stand fast therefore in the liberty
by which Christ has made us free
and do not be entangled again
with a yoke of bondage."
Galatians 5:1

THERE
IS

Life

"But the water that I shall give him
will become in him a fountain
of water springing up into
everlasting life."
John 4:14

THERE
IS

Kindness

"That in the ages to come
He might show
the exceeding riches
of His grace in His kindness
toward us in Christ Jesus."
Ephesians 2:7

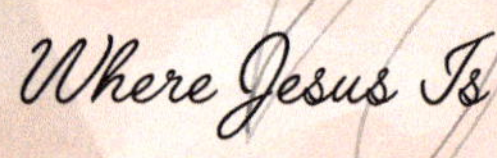

THERE
IS

Wisdom

"In whom are hidden
all the treasures
of wisdom and knowledge."
Colossians 2:3

THERE
IS

Mercy

"Keep yourselves
in the love of God,
looking for the mercy
of our Lord Jesus Christ
unto eternal life."
Jude 1:21

THERE
IS

Blessing

"Blessed be the God and Father
of our Lord Jesus Christ,
who has blessed us
with every spiritual blessing
in the heavenly places in Christ."
Ephesians 1:3

THERE
IS

Victory

"But thanks be to God,
who gives us the victory
through our Lord Jesus Christ."
1 Corinthians 15:57

THERE
IS

Fellowship

"God is faithful,
by whom you were called
into the fellowship of His Son,
Jesus Christ our Lord."
1 Corinthians 1:9

THERE
IS

Fruit

"Being filled with the fruits
of righteousness
which are by Jesus Christ,
to the glory and praise of God."
Philippians 1:11

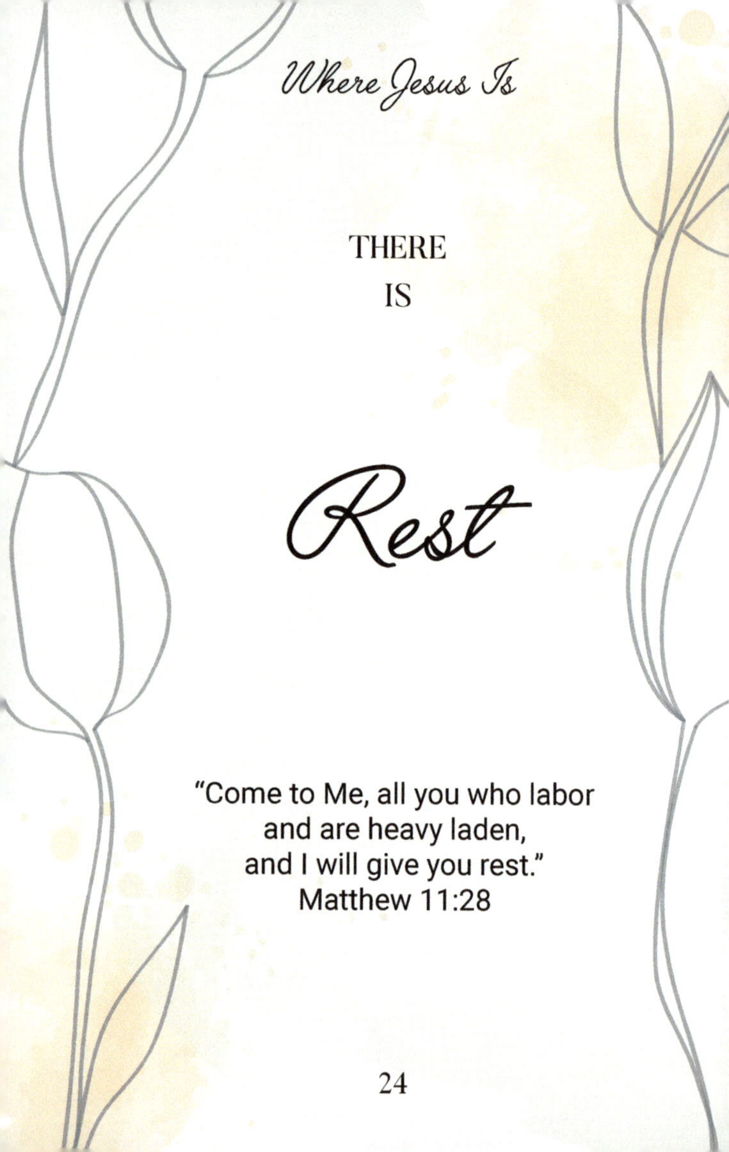

THERE
IS

Rest

"Come to Me, all you who labor
and are heavy laden,
and I will give you rest."
Matthew 11:28

THERE
IS

Authority

"And Jesus came
and spoke to them, saying,
'All authority has been given to Me
in heaven and on earth.'"
Matthew 28:18

THERE
IS

Light

"I have come as a light
into the world,
that whoever believes in Me
should not abide in darkness."
John 12:46

THERE
IS

Abundance

"I have come
that they may have life,
and that they may
have it more abundantly."
John 10:10

THERE
IS

Gentleness

"Now I, Paul, myself am pleading
with you by the meekness
and gentleness of Christ—who in
presence am lowly among you, but
being absent am bold toward you."
2 Corinthians 10:1

THERE

IS

Salvation

"Nor is there salvation in any
other, for there is no other name
under heaven given among men
by which we must be saved."
Acts 4:12

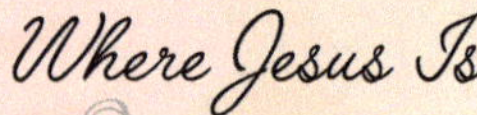

THERE
IS

Praise

"Saying: "I will declare Your name to My brethren; In the midst of the assembly I will sing praise to You.""
Hebrews 2:12

The Designer

Kourtney is a graphic designer/creative,
living in Atlanta, Georgia.
She is passionate to produce images that
challenge the average concept of life.
In this book, she provides the backdrop for
Words that lead people to a better
understanding of God, themselves,
and others.

The Editor

After writing for thirty years, Fran shared her articles in booklets by desktop publishing, started blogging at God's Grace ~ God's Glory in 2011, reproduced and published Bogatzky's, A Golden Treasury as her first eBook on Amazon. Since 2016, she has published thirteen of her non-fiction books for the Christian life and spiritual growth, seven in the series Little Books about the Magnitude of God. She writes from the love and fellowship of her heavenly Father and Christ through twenty-eight years of caring for grandchildren, her father with cancer, her mother who had Alzheimer's Disease and her husband, Jerry, who was an amputee with diabetes and heart disease. Since his death in June 2020, she has devoted her time to caring for the members of her church family, and leading women in small prayer groups. She continues to write of God's grace, proclaiming His kingdom for His glory and the joy of His children.

Series from Father and Family Books

Little Books About the Magnitude of God
FIRST THINGS That Last FOREVER
TWO FULL PLATES ~
Learning to be a Caregiver
The Garden of GOD`S Word ~
The Purpose and Delight of BIBLE STUDY
The LITTLE BOAT
and other Short Stories of GOD`S GRACE
GOD Is Our Goal

What the Holy Bible Says
What the Holy BIBLE Says About LIGHT
What the Holy BIBLE Says About the WORD
of GOD

OTHER BOOKS
Prayers That Bring the House Down
One Month to Live ~ A Fathers`s Last Words
A Broad Review of Andrew Murray`s Humility
Child Keeping ~ God`s Blessing to Parents
Beyond a mere Christianity
Godly CONTENTment

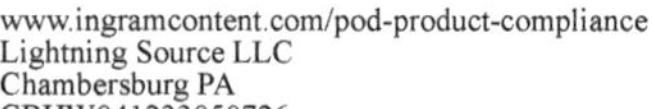